G. Scott. Sc.ᵗ

HANNAH SNELL,
The Female Soldier &c

THE AUGUSTAN REPRINT SOCIETY

THE
Female Soldier;

Or, The Surprising

LIFE *and* ADVENTURES

O F

H A N N A H   S N E L L

(1750)

Introduction by
DIANNE DUGAW

Publication Number 257
WILLIAM ANDREWS CLARK MEMORIAL LIBRARY
University of California, Los Angeles
1989

Introduction © 1989 by The William Andrews Clark Memorial Library
University of California, Los Angeles
2520 Cimarron Street
Los Angeles, California 90018
Telephone: (213) 731-8529

Designed and printed by The Castle Press
Pasadena, California

INTRODUCTION

PERHAPS THE MOST surprising fact about eighteenth-century female soldiers and sailors is their frequency, not only in fiction but in history as well. Heroines such as Hannah Snell actually surface as commonplace, particularly in works catering to the lower classes. Thus, street ballads sing of female drummers, valiant maidens, and women warriors.[1] Theatrical interludes depict masquerading Pollys who accompany their Jack Tars through plots that enlace the triumphs of virtuous love and the nation's glory.[2] Prose biographies tell the conventionalized stories of actual female warriors: Mrs. Christian Davies, Deborah Sampson, Maria Knowles, Mary Anne Talbot, "blue-eyed Patty," Defoe's female pirates Anne Bonny and Mary Read.[3] Of these last, the prose "histories," *The Female Soldier; Or, The Surprising Life and Adventures of Hannah Snell* is a particularly interesting example—a fascinating middlebrow formulation of a lower-class heroine and her ballad-like story.

In 1750 the London printer Robert Walker, an important early newspaper publisher,[4] presented his readers with two anonymous versions of *The Female Soldier*, the 46-page unillustrated octavo reproduced here and a more developed 187-page book which included engraved illustrations. Both accounts bear the same title and the same 1750 imprint. Indeed, they are short and long versions—less and more expensive productions, one supposes—of a single text.[5] The longer version has more adventures, which are developed in greater detail and with more novelistic description and didactic comment. Both claim to be factual accounts gotten firsthand from the "Female Soldier" herself, the masquerading Hannah Snell, unlettered[6] daughter of a Worcester hosier.

While the outlines of her "life and adventures" are highly conventionalized—in some ways more predictable than "surprising"—Hannah Snell was a real person.[7] What is known

[v]

of her early life seems derived almost entirely from the 1750 narrative: She was born in Worcester in 1723, married in 1744, and dressed as a man in 1745 to join the army in search of her missing husband, whom she eventually discovered had been executed. Under the name James Gray, she saw action in both the army and the navy from 1745 to 1750. Serving as cook, assistant steward, and common seaman aboard ship, she also fought intermittently on land, suffering severe wounds during the siege of the French stronghold at Pondicherry, India. Through it all, she maintained her masquerade, "as good a Man as any Seaman on board" (19). When her ship's crew was paid off at Gravesend in 1750, Snell made known her adventures, which Robert Walker quickly printed up as *The Female Soldier*.

The Female Soldier represents an early modern preoccupation with cross-dressing in general and women soldiers in particular.[8] This preoccupation, which had long currency in lower-class ballads, for a time attracted a wider and more sophisticated audience. In that circular way that popularity works, Walker's publication of *The Female Soldier* simultaneously resulted from and contributed to this wider currency of the Female Warrior idea. Abridgments of *The Female Soldier* immediately appeared in the *Gentleman's Magazine* and the *Scots Magazine*.[9] Within months of Walker's two versions, *The Female Soldier* had been translated into Dutch.[10] The heroine herself appeared on stage at Sadler's Wells, where, dressed in her regimentals, she performed various of her military exercises.[11] With the demise of her entr'acte career, Snell moved to Wapping, where she opened a public house identified by the sign of "The Female Warrior." After several decades of celebrity, Hannah Snell eventually declined both in health and in fortune and was removed to Bethlehem Hospital, where she died in 1792.[12]

Despite the protectionist affidavit on Walker's behalf in its preface, *The Female Soldier* was quickly taken up by other printers, and Snell's story made its way into the packs and pockets of readers well below Walker's original audience. Already in the 1750s a 24-page abridgment was published as a chapbook by the famous Bow Church Yard publishers William and Cluer Dicey.[13] Eventually, 24-page and 16-page versions of Snell's story appeared under the imprint of chapbook printers as far away as provincial York and even Northampton, Massachusetts.[14] For the lower-class readers of such chapbooks, Hannah Snell would have been commonplace rather than eccentric, a heroine in a long line of ballad female warriors.[15]

But Walker's biography widened the audience for the idea of female soldiering considerably, for it brought the Female Warrior to a middlebrow readership. If Snell's story quickly found a lower-class chapbook market, it also appeared as eccentric news in the *Gentleman's Magazine* and sold in Walker's leatherbound versions of 46 and 187 pages. These were not cheap, lower-class publications. Walker's books and the news accounts drawn from them are directed to an audience apparently unaccustomed to the Female Warrior idea. In these accounts, a female warrior like Snell is more than a little curious.

One discerns two not always congruous strains in Walker's rendition of Snell's adventures: on the one hand, a natively intrepid heroine and adventure-packed story in the style of lower-class street ballads, and on the other, a narrative voice from a very different context shaping and trying to make sense of this character and her life. The historical Hannah Snell — a matter-of-factly gritty woman with a resilience reminiscent of Moll Flanders — can be inferred from the "facts" of her tumultuous life. Overlaying this "truth," the middlebrow and ambivalent narrator interprets Snell as an example of "Heroinism" (2) for "the Fair Sex" (41), while simultaneously marveling at "the Oddity of her Conduct for preserving her Virtue" (iii). The narrator's reading identifies her in novelistic and sentimental terms as "one of the tender Sex, who are afraid of Shaddows, and shudders at the Pressage of a Dream" (15); and yet Snell's *story* presents a life of manifestly forceful and direct actions. The conjunction of these two strains creates in *The Female Soldier* a fascinating and tellingly incongruent texture.

At its outset, Hannah Snell's story fits the long-standing ballad pattern: a loving lower-class woman sets out in disguise to find her beloved, who has enlisted. Of course, the knavery of Snell's husband fits not at all into this kind of ballad, where soldier-sweethearts are almost invariably just such heroes as deserve such dauntless heroines. But other features of Snell's narrative call to mind the popular ballads. Snell takes up her transvestite disguise with unconcerned matter-of-factness: her disguise and her enlistment together take up a single sentence (7). In similar fashion, ballad heroines simply don "seamen's shew" or march off "in Mans array,"[16] and nothing more is said. Then, like many a ballad heroine, Snell "willingly took her Turn at the Pump" and "performed the several Offices of a common Sailor" (13). *The Female Sailor Bold* sings of a heroine who, with the same nautical industriousness, "would run to the top gallant-sail, did reef and steer we're told."[17] In another ballad, *The Female Sea-Captain*, the heroine likewise "bravely . . . learned the Mariners Art."[18]

Other of Snell's adventures have their ballad parallels. Her "Shot in the Groin" (15) has its counterpart in the wounding of balladry's "Young Nancy" "in the very heat of action," or in the equally gender-charged maiming of the female soldier of *The Lancashire Heros* who received "a large bullet . . . Which took off her left breast."[19] Like Snell, ballad female warriors court the ladies, as we hear in *The Female Sailor*: "For when in port, she was as jolly as a sailor could be, / Her grog she would drink, and kiss the girls merrily."[20] Similarly, *The Female Soldier* gives—almost in ballad terms—further episodes of sexual ambiguity created by Snell's transvestism. When the narrator says that "It is here worthy of Observation, that this Woman should lay three Nights with two different Men" without discovery (29), ballad lines immediately come to mind. *The Valiant Maiden*, for example, declares: "Nothing would put this fair maid in a fright, / She lay betwixt two Men every Night."[21]

Nevertheless, much in the discourse of Walker's *The Female Soldier* sets it apart from lower-class ballads and chapbooks. Key to the difference is the incredulous and editorializing narrator, who struggles throughout to interpret unfamiliar and —one suspects—unpalatable events, behaviors, sentiments, and themes. Speaking to the novel-reading—as opposed to the ballad-singing—public, *The Female Soldier* brings to Snell's lower-class story the codes and expectations of a different audience. Looking for conventions and precedents, the narrator places Hannah Snell in the epic company of the Amazons and of Cleopatra and Semiramis on the one hand, and the pastoral band of "*Arcadian* Shepherdesses" on the other (2).

And yet, the summoning of heroic prototypes — lofty "*Rarae Aves in Terris*" (1) — is actually short-lived. Rather, it is the ethos of the newly emergent Richardsonian novel that ultimately informs *The Female Soldier*. Indeed, the narrator ringingly concludes Snell's story by saluting her (40–41) as "the real *Pamella*" whose "Adventures and Virtues" surpass those of Richardson's "romantick" and "counterfeit" heroine. Unlike Pamela Andrews, Hannah Snell is "real Flesh and Blood." But it is not just quality that dictates this preference for "the real *Pamella*" but quantity as well. Richardson's Pamela kept at bay only a single squire. "[O]ur Heroine," by contrast, is for the narrator an epic "*Pamella*," preserving "her Chastity by the most virtuous Stratagems," even "in the midst of thousands of the Martial Gentry" on land and "hardy resolute Tars" at sea, "who soon would have batter'd down the Fort of her Virtue, had they discovered that *James Gray* was Mrs. *Hannah Snell*."

But, of course, Hannah's story is not really Pamela's at all — the narrator's Richardsonian projections notwithstanding. Unlike Pamela, Hannah plays, not "the Fort," but the warrior, exposing in her masquerade the gender-based construction of heroism in both stories. Unlike Pamela, Hannah remains in a lower-class context whose desperate brutishness seeps up through the language of pastoral elevation, sexual titillation, and ill-fitted moralizing that encases her narrative. *The Female Soldier* is an illuminating text: a narrative fabric of fascinating social and aesthetic incongruities. With a mixture of admiration and uneasiness, Walker brings before his novel-buying public a heroine straight from the lower class, a representative of both its experience and its discourse. Like the heroine of many a ballad, Hannah Snell lived out a lower-class story that had been told again and again in the century before her. As *The Woman Warrior*, a ballad of the 1690s, exuberantly exhorted:

Let the Females attend,
To the Lines which are penn'd,
    For here I shall give a Relation;
Of a Young marry'd Wife,
Who did venture her Life,
    For a Soldier, a Soldier she went from the Nation.[22]

University of Colorado at Boulder

1. For versions of these ballads, see *The Female Drummer* in an Edinburgh chapbook printed by J. Morren ca. 1800–1820, in Harvard University, Houghton Library, 25252.19, chapbook 31; *The Valiant Maiden* on an American broadside ca. 1800, in Brown University, John Hay Library, Harris 40361; and *The Woman Warrier* on a London broadside printed for C. Bates ca. 1709–12, in Harvard, Houghton, 25242.68/pEB–B65H, vol. 2, fol. 307r.

2. Some of these can be found among the Larpent Play Manuscripts in the Huntington Library. Richard Sheridan's *The Camp* (1778) is one of the few well-known examples.

3. See *The Life and Adventures of Mrs. Christian Davies* (London: R. Montagu, 1740); [Herman Mann], *The Female Review: Or, Memoirs of an American Young Lady* (Dedham, [Mass.]: Nathaniel and Benjamin Heaton, [1797]; reprints, Boston: J. K. Wiggin and W. P. Lunt, 1866, and Tarrytown, N.Y.: W. Abbatt, 1916); *The Surprising Life and Adventures of Maria Knowles* (Newcastle: M. Angus, [ca. 1798]), in Newberry Library, Case Y148.157, vol. 1; *The Intrepid Female: Or, Surprising Life and Adventures of Mary-Anne Talbot, otherwise John Taylor*, in *Kirby's Wonderful and Eccentric Museum*, 6 vols. (London: R. S. Kirby, 1820), 2:160–225 (*The Intrepid Female* was published separately as a chapbook in the first decade of the nineteenth century); *The life and surprising adventures of blue-eyed Patty, the valiant female soldier* (Wolverhampton: J. Hately, [ca. 1800]), in Cleveland Public Library, John G. White Collection, W381. 521F779m; and Daniel Defoe, *A General History of the Pyrates*, ed. Manuel Schonhorn (London: J. M. Dent, 1972), 153–65.

4. For information on Walker, see Henry R. Plomer et al., *A Dictionary of the Printers and Booksellers Who Were at Work in England, Scotland, and Ireland from 1726 to 1775* (Oxford: Bibliographical Society, 1932), 252–53.

5. There has been some confusion in the catalogues because Walker issued two separate versions of Snell's life in the same year. This facsimile of the shorter version is reproduced from the copy in the New York State Library at Albany, and I am indebted to Christine M. Beauregard of Manuscripts and Special Collections for her help in securing it. Other copies of the shorter version can be found in the Newberry Library, the University of Illinois at Urbana-Champaign, and Cambridge University. Copies of the longer version are at the

William Andrews Clark Memorial Library, Princeton University, and the British Library. In 1893 M. M. Dowie [Mrs. M. M. (D.) Norman] included her own much-abbreviated telling of Snell's story in *Women Adventurers: . . . The Lives of Madame Velazquez, Hannah Snell, Mary Anne Talbot, and Mrs. Christian Davies* (London: T. Fisher Unwin, 1893), 59–131.

6. According to *The Female Soldier*, Snell "did not while she was at School learn to write, yet she made a tolerable Progress in the other Part of Education common to her Sex, and could read exceeding well" (3).

7. See the entry on her in *The Dictionary of National Biography* 18:613–14.

8. For discussion of female soldiers and their place in early modern experience, see Dianne Dugaw, *Warrior Women and Popular Balladry 1650–1850* (Cambridge: Cambridge University Press, forthcoming 1989), and Julie Wheelwright, *Amazons and Military Maids* (London: Pandora Press, 1989).

9. "Some account of Hannah Snell, the Female Soldier," *Gentleman's Magazine* 20 (July 1750): 291–93. The same "account" appears in the *Scots Magazine* 12 (July 1750): 330–32.

10. The Dutch version of Snell's *Adventures* is *De vrouwelyke soldaat of de verbazende levensgevallen van Anna Snell* (Amsterdam: Gerrit de Groot, 1750). I am indebted to Julie Wheelwright for this reference.

11. Dennis Arundell, *The Story of Sadler's Wells, 1683–1977,* 2d extended ed. (Newton Abbott, Eng.: David and Charles, 1978), 17.

12. *Dictionary of National Biography* 18:613–14.

13. A copy of this chapbook is in the National Library of Scotland in Edinburgh and bears the date 1756 and the Bow Church Yard imprint of William and Cluer Dicey. For discussion of the Diceys, see Victor E. Neuburg, "The Diceys and the Chapbook Trade," *Library*, 5th ser., 24 (1969): 219–31.

14. See *The Surprising Life and Adventures of Hannah Snell alias James Gray; or the Female Warrior*, a 24-page chapbook published in York in 1809 by J. Kendrew, in Harvard, Houghton, 25276.43.13; and *The Widow in Masquerade*, a 16-page chapbook published in Northampton, Massachusetts, in 1809, in the American Antiquarian Society, 19232.

15. The earliest English Female Warrior ballad is *The Valarous Acts performed at Gaunt, By the brave Bonny Lass Mary Ambree*, a song

that was popular about 1600 and continued to be sung and reprinted until the nineteenth century. It has been ascribed to William Elderton, though his authorship is by no means certain. For a text, see *The Bagford Ballads*, ed. Joseph W. Ebsworth, 2 vols. (Hertford: Stephen Austin, for the Ballad Society, 1878), 1:308–15. For authorship, see Hyder E. Rollins, "William Elderton: Elizabethan Actor and Ballad-Writer," *Studies in Philology* 17 (1920): 236.

16. *The Merchant of Bristol's Daughter* (1791), in Harvard, Houghton, 25274.2, vol. 8, chapbook 9; *An Admirable New Northern Story* (ca. 1690), in *The Euing Collection of English Broadside Ballads in the Library of the University of Glasgow* (Glasgow: University of Glasgow Publications, 1971), 9.

17. From a broadside printed in London by J. Catnach ca. 1836, in University of Kentucky, Broadside Collection, 5:30.

18. From a London chapbook of the mid–eighteenth century, in Harvard, Houghton, 25252.6, Garland 55.

19. A broadside of *Wounded Nancy's Return* was printed in London by J. Davenport ca. 1780 and can be found in W. H. Logan, *A Pedlar's Pack of Ballads and Songs* (Edinburgh: William Paterson, 1869; reprint, Detroit: Singing Tree Press, 1968), 94–100; text quotations on 97–98. A broadside of *The Lancashire Heros* was printed in Liverpool by W. Armstrong ca. 1800 and can be found in the Library of Congress, Rare Book Division, Ballads, 1790–1830, item 174.

20. From a broadside printed in Boston in the 1830s by L. Deming, in the American Antiquarian Society, Uncatalogued Ballads.

21. For *The Valiant Maiden*, see note 1.

22. From Thomas D'Urfey's *Wit and Mirth: or Pills to purge Melancholy*, 6 vols. (London: W. Pearson, 1719–20), 5:8.

BIBLIOGRAPHICAL NOTE

The Female Soldier (1750) is reproduced in facsimile from a copy in the New York State Library, Albany (Shelf Mark: N/396.09/S671). The engraving is reproduced from the copy of the longer version of *The Female Soldier* (1750) in the William Andrews Clark Memorial Library (Shelf Mark: *PR3291/F328).

Snell, Hannah.

THE
Female Soldier;

Or, The Surprising

LIFE *and* ADVENTURES

O F

HANNAH SNELL,

Born in the CITY of *Worcester,*

Who took upon herself the Name of *James Gray*; and, being deserted by her Husband, put on Mens Apparel, and travelled to *Coventry* in quest of him, where she enlisted in Col. *Guise's* Regiment of Foot, and marched with that Regiment to *Carlisle,* in the Time of the Rebellion in *Scotland*; shewing what happened to her in that City, and her Desertion from that Regiment.

A L S O

A Full and True ACCOUNT of her enlisting afterwards into *Fraser's* Regiment of Marines, then at *Portsmouth*; and her being draughted out of that Regiment, and sent on board the *Swallow* Sloop of War, one of Admiral *Boscawen's* Squadron, then bound for the *East-Indies.* With the many Vicissitudes of Fortune she met with during that Expedition, particularly at the Siege of *Pondicherry,* where she received Twelve Wounds. Likewise, the surprising Accident by which she came to hear of the Death of her faithless Husband, who she went in quest of.

T O G E T H E R

With an ACCOUNT of what happened to her in the Voyage to *England,* in the *Eltham* Man of War. The whole containing the most surprizing Incidents that have happened in any preceeding Age; wherein is laid open all her Adventures, in Mens Cloaths, for near five Years, without her Sex being ever discovered.

L O N D O N:

Printed for, and Sold by R. WALKER, the Corner of *Elliot's- Court,* in the *Little Old-Bailey.* 1750. Price One Shilling.)

lporbent/45 ld june 1750

TO THE

PUBLICK.

*N*Otwithstanding the surprizing Adventures of this our British Heroine, of whom the following Pages fully and impartially treat; yet the Oddity of her Conduct for preserving her Virtue was such, that it demands not only Respect, but Admiration; and as there is nothing to be found in the following Sheets, but what is Matter of Fact, it merits the Countenance and Approbation of every Inhabitant of this great Isle, especially the Fair Sex, for whom this Treatise is chiefly intended; and the Truth of which being confirmed by our Heroines Affidavit, made before the Right Hon. the Lord Mayor, the said Affidavit is hereunto annexed, in order to prevent the Publick from being imposed upon by fictitious Accounts.

*H*ANNAH SNELL, *born in the City of* Worcester, *in the Year of our Lord* 1723, *and who took upon her the Name of* James Gray, *maketh Oath, and saith, That she this Deponent served his present Majesty King* George, *as a Soldier and Sailor, from the* 27th *of* November, *One Thousand Seven Hundred and Forty-five, to the* 9th *of this Instant* June.

June, *and entered herself as a Marine in Capt.* Graham's *Company in Col.* Frafer's *Regiment, and went on board the* Swallow, *his Majesty's Sloop of War, to the* East-Indies, *belonging to Admiral* Boscawen's *Squadron, where this Deponent was present at the Siege of* Pondicherry, *and all the other Sieges during that Expedition, in which she received Twelve Wounds, some of which were dangerous, and was put into the Hospital for Cure of the same, and returned into* England *in the* Eltham *Man of War, Capt.* Lloyd *Commander, without the least Discovery of her Sex.*

And this Deponent further maketh Oath, and faith, That she has delivered to Robert Walker, *Printer, in the* Little Old-Bailey, London, *a full and true Account of the many surprizing Incidents, and wonderful Hardships she underwent during the Time she was in his Majesty's Service as aforesaid, to be by him printed and published.*

And this Deponent lastly faith, That she has not given the least Hint of her surprifing Adventures to any other Person, nor will she, this Deponent, give any the least Account thereof, to any Person whatsoever, to be printed or published, save and except the above-mentioned Robert Walker.

Sworn before me this 27th Day
   of *June,* 1750, at *Goldfmith's*
   Hall, London,

   J. BLACHFORD, Mayor.

Witnefs
    Sufannah Gray,
Sifter of the said Hannah Snell.
    T. Edwards.

           Her
           Hannah x Snell,
           Mark.

                        T H E

THE
LIFE
AND
ADVENTURES
OF
Hannah Snell, &c.

IN this daſtardly Age of the World, when Effeminacy and Debauchery have taken Place of the Love of Glory, and that noble Ardor after war-like Exploits, which flowed in the Boſoms of our Anceſtors, genuine Heroiſm, or rather an extraordinary Degree of Cou-rage, are Prodigies among Men. What Age, for Inſtance, produces a *Charles* of *Sweden*, a *Marl-borough*, or a Prince *Eugene?* Theſe are *Raræ Aves in Terris,* and when they appear, they ſeem to be particularly deſigned by Heaven, for protecting the Rights of injured Nations, againſt foreign Oppreſ-

ſion.

fion, fecuring the Privileges of Innocence from the dire Affault of Prey and Rapine ; and, in a Word, vindicating the common Prerogatives of human Nature, from the fatal Effects of brutal Rage, the love of Conqueft, and an infatiable Luft after Power. The amazing Benefit arifing to Mankind from fuch illuftrious and exalted Characters, is, perhaps, the principal Reafon why they attract the Eyes, and command the Attention of all who hear of them, even in Quarters of the World far remote from their Influence and Sphere of Action : Why they are the Subjects of the Poets Song, the Founders of the Hiftorian Narration, and the Objects of the Painters Pencil ; all which have a Tendency to tranfmit their Names with immortal Glory to lateft Ages, and eternize their Memories, when their Bodies are mouldred into Duft, and mingled with their Parent Earth. Perhaps their Rarity may alfo contribute, in a great Meafure, to that Efteem and Veneration, which the World thinks fit to pay them : But fure if Heroifm, Fortitude, and a Soul equal to all the glorious Acts of War and Conqueft, are Things fo rare, and fo much admired among Men ; how much rarer, and confequently how much more are they to be admired among Women ? In fhort, we may on this Occafion, without any Hyperbole, ufe the Words of *Solomon*, and fay, *One Man among a thoufand have I found, but among Women not fo.* However, tho' Courage and warlike Expeditions, are not the Provinces by the World allotted to Women fince the Days of tho *Amazons*, yet the female Sex is far from being deftitute of Heroinifm. *Cleopatra* headed a noble Army againft *Mark Anthony*, the greateft Warrior of his Time. *Semiramis* was not inferior to her in Courage. The *Arcadian* Shepherdeffes are as memorable for their Contempt of Danger as their darling and beloved Swains. But among all our Heroines, none comes more immediately under our Cognizance, nor, perhaps, more merits our Attention than the remarkable

Hannah

Hannah Snell, whofe Hiftory is highly interefting, both on Account of the Variety of amazing Incidents, and the untainted Veracity with which it is attended. Some People guided rather by the Suggeftions of Caprice, than the Dictates of Reafon and a found Underftanding, have foolifhly imagin'd, that Perfons of low and undiftinguifhed Births, hardly ever rais'd themfelves to the Summit of Glory and Renown ; but they will find themfelves widely miftaken, when they reflect on a *Kouli-Kan*, a *Cromwell*, and many others I could mention. But if this Obfervation had the fmalleft Foundation either in Nature or the Courfe of human Experience, from the moft remote, to the prefent Age, yet its Force does by no Means extend to *Hannah Snell*, the Heroine of the fubfequent Narrative : For though her immediate Progenitors were but low in the World, when compared with Dukes, Earls and Generals, yet fhe had the Seeds of Heroifm, Courage and Patriotifm transferr'd to her from her Anceftors, as will appear from the following Account of her Genealogy.

HANNAH SNELL, was born in *Fryer-Street*, in the Parifh of St. *Hollen's*, in the City of *Worcefter*, on the 23d Day of *April*, 1723. Her Parents, tho' not immenfely Rich by the hereditary Gifts of Fortune, yet fecured a Competency, which not only placed them above Contempt, but alfo enabled them to bring up, and educate a numerous Family, none of whom have mifcarried for want either of fufficient Learning from Mafters, or falutary Advices and virtuous Examples from their Parents. And though Mrs. *Hannah Snell* did not while fhe was at School learn to write. yet fhe made a tolerable Progrefs in the other Part of Education common to her Sex, and could read exceeding well.

THOUGH

THOUGH the Father of our Heroine was no more than a *Hofier* and *Dyer*, yet he was the Son of the illuftrious Capt. Lieut. *Sam. Snell*, for fo I may or rather muft call him, fince with Intrepidity he ftood the Brunt of the Wars in the latter End of King *William*'s Reign, fignalized himfelf at the taking of *Dunkirk*, and ferved faithfully in the *Englifh* Army during Queen *Anne*'s Wars.

THIS Captain Lieutenant *Snell*, the Grandfather of our Heroine, enter'd as a Volunteer in King *William*'s Reign, and in the Beginning of Queen *Anne*'s Wars, was at the taking of *Dunkirk* under the Duke of *Marlborough*, where the Captain Lieutenant was killed by a Shot fired through the Wicket by the Governor; upon which he fired, and killed the Governor. When the Duke was informed thereof, he called him, and asked him what Preferment he defired; his Anfwer was, that he chofe to accept of that Commiffion, which was become vacant by the Death of the Captain Lieutenant, which he was immediately preferr'd to, and took upon him the Command as fuch. After the Surrender of *Dunkirk*, where he received feveral dangerous Wounds, he returned to *England*, where he had the proffer of a very handfome Penfion in *Chelfea College*; but coveting frefh Glory, and new Trophies of Conqueft, be intreated of his Grace, that he would permit him once more to go Abroad with him, that he might have an Opportunity of fignalizing his Valour, againft the avowed Enemies of his Country. This his Requeft his Grace complied with, and at the Battle of *Malplaquet* he received a mortal Wound, from whence he was carried to *Ghent*, where he died: This laft, was the twenty-fecond bloody Battle in which he had been engaged, and which he generoufly launched out into upon the fublime Motives, Liberty and Property. This Gentleman's Character muft appear the more fublime, when we obferve how he advanced himfelf by

Merit

Merit from a private *Cadit* to the Rank he held
at his Death; and had it not been for his over-
modeſt and generous Sentiments, he might have
been preferr'd to a much higher Rank; but the
Engliſhman prevail'd above Self-Intereſt.

The Son of this illuſtrious Man of whom we
have here treated, and Father of our Heroine,
was poſſeſſed of many excellent Gifts, particularly
Courage, for which he was diſtinguiſhed; yet
never had an Opportunity of diſplaying his Bravery in the Field of Battle, his Genius leading him
another Way, to wit, Trade, into which he entered very young, and proſpered in the World,
married to his liking, and in a few Years ſaw himſelf the Father of nine promiſing Children, three
of which were Sons, and ſix Daughters, all of
whom ſave one Daughter, were either Soldiers
or Sailors, or intermarried with them. The
eldeſt of the Sons, *Samuel Snell*, incapable of
Reſtraint, and void of all Fear, liſted himſelf a Soldier in Lord *Robert Manners's* Company in the firſt
Regiment of Foot-Guards, commanded by his
Royal Highneſs the Duke of *Cumberland*; when he
was draughted to go for *Flanders*, where he received
his mortal Wound at the Battle of *Fontenoy*; and
being ſent to the Hoſpital at *Doway*, he there
expired.

Tho' the Daughters were, by thoſe who knew
them, accounted aimable Women, both on Account of their Perſons and their Virtue; yet I ſhall
paſs over the Characters of five of them in Silence,
and only take Notice of that of *Hannah*, the young-
eſt of them but one, who is the Heroine of this
Subject. It is a common Thing to obſerve a Family diſperſed, when the Heads of that Family are
either laid in their Graves, or by accidental Calamities rendered incapable of ſupporting it longer.
Accordingly, when the Father and Mother of

Hannah

Hannah died, *Hannah* came up to *London*, and arrived in Town on *Chriſtmas-Day*, 1740, and reſided for ſome Time, with her Siſter in *Wapping*.

SOME Time after ſhe came to *London*, ſhe contracted an Acquaintance with one *James Summs*, a Sailor, who was a *Dutchman*; this Acquaintance was gradually improved into a Familiarity, and this Familiarity ſoon created a mutual, tho' not a criminal Paſſion; for in a little Time, *Summs* made his Addreſſes to her as a Lover, and gained her Conſent, and was married to her at the *Fleet*, on the ſixth Day of *January*, 1743-4. But all his Promiſes of Friendſhip, proved Inſtances of the higheſt Perfidy, and he turn'd out the worſt and moſt unnatural of Huſbands. Since, tho' ſhe had Charms enough to captivate the Heart, and ſecure the Affection of any reaſonable Man, yet ſhe was deſpiſed and contemned by her Huſband, who not only kept criminal Company with other Women of the baſeſt Characters, but alſo made away with her Things, in Order to ſupport his Luxury, and the daily Expences of his Whores. During this unlucky Period of the Husband's Debauchery, ſhe poor Woman proved with Child, and at the ſame Time felt all the Shocks of Poverty, without expoſing her Neceſſities to her neareſt Friends. But at laſt, her Pregnancy laid the Foundation for her paſſing through all the Scenes, thro' which ſhe has wandered; for when ſhe was ſeven Months gone with Child, her perfidious Huſband finding himſelf deeply involv'd in Debt, made an Elopement from her. Notwithſtanding theſe her Calamities, ſhe patiently bore herſelf up under them, and in two Months after her Huſband's Departure was delivered of a Daughter which lived no more than ſeven Months, and was decently interred at her own Expence at St. *George*'s Pariſh in *Middleſex*.

FROM

FROM the Time of her Husband's Elopement till the Time she put on Man's Cloaths, she continued with her Sister, who is married to one *James Gray*, a House Carpenter, in *Ship-street*, *Wapping*, and from whence she took her Departure unknown to any, and was never heard of until her Return; and with whom she now dwells.

As she was now free from all the Ties arising from Nature and Consanguinity; she thought herself privileged to roam in quest of the Man, who, without Reason, had injured her so much; for there are no Bounds to be set either to Love, Jealousy or Hatred, in the female Mind. That she might execute her Designs with the better Grace, and the more Success, she boldly commenced a Man, at least in her Dress, and no doubt she had a Right to do so, since she had the real Soul of a Man in her Breast. Dismay'd at no Accidents, and giving a full Scope to the genuine Bent of her Heart, she put on a Suit of her Brother-in-Law, Mr. *James Gray*'s, Cloaths, assumed his Name, and set out on the 23d of *November*, 1745, and travelled to *Coventry*, with a View of finding her Husband, where she enlisted on the 27th of the said Month of *November*, in General *Guise*'s Regiment, and in the Company belonging to Captain *Miller*.

WITH this Regiment she marched from *Coventry* to *Carlisle*, where she learned her military Exercise, which she now performs with as much Skill and Dexterity as any Serjeant or Corporal in his Majesty's Service. But here, as Fortune is often a Foe to the Distressed, she met with a discouraging Circumstance; for her Serjeant, whose Name was *Davis*, having a criminal Inclination for a young Woman in that Town, looked upon this our Female Heroine, (a common Soldier in the Company) as a proper Person for assisting him in this his vicious Intrigue, therefore disclosed to her this Bosom Secret,

Secret, and defired her Endeavours in promoting this
End ; however, this open Difcovery caufed a fudden
Emotion in her Mind, her virtuous Soul abhorred
with a becoming Deteftation the criminal Intention;
yet to prevent the ill Confequences that fhe forefaw
muft enfue from a refufal of complying with his Requeft, fhe promifed to ufe her Endeavours in his
Behalf ; but inftead of acting the Pimp, fhe went
and difclofed the whole Matter to the young Woman, and warned her againft the impending Danger ; which Act of Virtue and Generofity in a
Soldier, gained her the Efteem and Confidence of
this young Woman, who took great delight in her
Company ; and feldom a Day paffed but they were
together, having cultivated an Intimacy and Friend-
fhip with each other : But *Davis* going one Day
to make his Addreffes to his Miftrefs, met with
an unexpected Repulfe, which unufual Treatment
made him fufpect our Female Soldier. Jealoufy
that Moment took Poffeffion of his guilty Breaft,
and he imagined, that inftead of befriending him
in his Amours, fhe had become his Rival, and had
gained her over to her Inclinations. Thefe Reflections troubled him much ; Revenge reigned triumphant in his Breaft, and how to punifh her was
his chief Aim : He took hold of the earlieft Opportunity, and accufed her before the commanding
Officer for Neglect of Duty, upon which fhe was
fentenced to receive fix hundred Lafhes, five hundred of which fhe received, having her Hands tied
to the Caftle Gates for a Crime which Nature put it
out of her Power to perpetrate, and had undergone
the Punifhment of the other Hundred, had it not
been for the Interceffion of fome of the Officers.
This fevere and unjuft Punifhment, reduced her
to a very low State, but notwithftanding this fevere Whipping, the Villain *Davis* bore her
an implacable Hatred, and ftrove all he could
to deprefs her, by putting her upon the hard-
eft and moft difficult Duties ; but fhe was moft
                                              tenderly

tenderly and affectionately regarded by her Female
Friend, who neglected nothing that might assure
her, she was neither unmindful nor ungrateful for
the Friendship she had shewed her. Soon after this,
a fresh and unforeseen Trouble presented itself;
there happened to come a fresh Recruit to the Regiment, a young Man whose Name was *George
Beck*, a Carpenter, born in *Worcester* City, that
had come to *London* in Quest of Business, and happened to lodge with her Brother and Sister, and
whom she left at her Brothers House when she went
off in Men's Cloaths, the Sight of whom troubled her
much, fearing she should be discovered by him; this,
together with the Serjeant's ill Treatment, inspired
her with a Resolution to desert; having carried this
her Intention to Maturity, she communicated the
same to her intimate Friend the young Woman,
who, tho' loth to lose the Company of such a Friend
and Companion, yielded to her Remonstrances, and
provided her with Money to bear her Charge in
her intended Flight.

Having gone so far with the Author of this Subject, I cannot refrain making a little Digression,
and making a few Reflections upon the melancholy
Prospect : What an Ocean of Troubles was this
unfortunate Woman involved in? Behold her in-
wardly looking back on the past Vicissitudes of her
Life, on an inhumane, ungrateful and faithless Husband, who had broke through all Engagements,
sacred and civil, and had drove her into all the
direful Troubles and Afflictions she was then involved in : Behold her tempted by a vicious Man,
to be aiding and assisting in carrying on an immo-
dest and abominable Intrigue ; but (being inspired
with virtuous and generous Sentiments) she proved
the Instrument of extracting Good out of Evil,
in discovering to the innocent Maid, where the
Net was spread for her, that she might guard her
self against the Adversary : Behold the Friend-

C   ship fhip that this virtuous Difcovery produced, it chained them together in the ftricteft Bonds of Love and Affection, which never quitted its hold, till forced thereto by a hard Fate : Behold her fufpected of fupplanting the Serjeant of his Mif-trefs, and the direful Effects his Jealoufy occafion-ed, having her Arms extended, and fixed to the City Gates, and there receive the Number of five hundred fevere Lafhes, as the Effects of a partial and unjuft Sentence : Behold her tender Flefh cut and mangled by thefe Scourgings, and the Pains and Agonies fhe fuffered : Behold in this her Dif-trefs, the friendly Sympathy and eager Affiftance of her female Friend, who adminiftred Relief to her under this her Dilemma : Behold the Commo-tions fhe felt upon perciving one in the Regiment whom fhe knew, and by whom fhe was afraid of being difcovered ; the bad Treatment fhe met with from the Serjeant, and what a Storm muft furround her upon her projecting the Means for an Efcape, and the moving Seperation 'twixt her and her Friend : The Rehearfal of fo many concurring Cir-cumftances of Adverfity, is fufficient to melt the moft ftoney Heart into a compaffionate Tendernefs for this our female Adventurer.

Having finifhed this Digreffion, I fhall begin where I left off. Upon her Defertion, fhe fet out on Foot for *Portfmouth*, and about a Mile out of *Carlifle*, exchanged her regimental Clothes for worfe, with fome People employed in cutting down Peafe. But Courage and Love, like impetuous Torrents, rage the more they are oppofed ; for *Hannah* whofe Breaft was actuated with both thefe Principles, had no fooner arrived at *Portfmouth*, than fhe found her Expectations difapointed : How-ever, whether Defpair or the Hopes of again meet-ing that unfaithful Man, who had made her the Mother of a helplefs Infant, actuated her Breaft and gave her Paffions a preternatural Spring. So it

was,

was, that she courageously inlisted herself in Captain *Graham*'s Company in Colonel *Fraser*'s Regiment, and soon after there was a Draught made, to go abroad in Admiral *Boscawen*'s Fleet, and she chanced to be one of the Number draughted, and went immediately on board the *Swallow* Sloop, Captain *Rosier*, Commander ; and when on board was observed to be handy in washing, as well as in dressing Victuals, for the Mess she first belonged to, and being thus remarkable, she was sollicited by *Richard Wyegate*, Lieutenant of Marines, to become one of their Mess, which she readily agreed to, as believing the Officers Mess, was better than the common Mens, and she acted in the Station of their Boy, and by her modest Deportment soon became a Favourite, drest their Victuals, washed and mended their Linnen. She was stationed (in Case of an Engagement) on the Quarter-Deck, and to fight at small Arms, and made one of the After-Guard ; she was obliged to keep watch four Hours on and four off, Day and Night, being often obliged to go aloft, and altho' unexperienced with these Kind of Hardships, soon became expert in the Business.

On their first setting sail, they enjoyed as fine Weather, and as fair Winds as could possibly be wished for, to convey a Ship safely and expeditiously from one Harbour to another. But no sooner were they arrived in the Bay of *Biscay* than the Scene was altered ; their favourable Weather converted into a dismal Hurricane, and their smooth placed Ocean, changed into Billows, which threaten'd them with immediate Death, by this Moment raising them to the Clouds, and in the next plunging them, as it were, to the Centre of the Earth. The Danger may be easily estimated, from the Circumstance, for the *Swallow* was as strong and well built a Vessel, as any belonging to his Majesty's Navy of her Burden ; yet such was the Stress

C 2 of

of Weather, that she sprung her Main-maft, and loft
not only the Gib-Boom, but alfo two Top-mafts.
After they had for feveral Days been beat about in
this imminent Danger, they with great Difficulty
arrived in the Port of *Lisbon*, which was great Joy
to them, after having fuffered fo much in the Bay
of *Bifcay*, where every Moment they had been in
danger of being fwallowed up in the vaft Abyfs.
In this Port, which to them was like a fafe Afylum,
or Sanctuary, to a Man purfued by a hungry
and enraged Lyon, they continued three Weeks ;
becaufe the Veffel was fo damaged, that the
Number of Hands employed in refitting her could
not do it fooner.

HERE they found the *Vigilant* Man of War,
which was likewife much damaged in the Storm in
the Bay of *Bifcay*, being one of the Fleet that fail'd
from *Portfmouth* with them.

WHILE she was afhore at *Lisbon*, with her Mafter, she was quartered at one Mrs. *Poore*'s a Punch-
Houfe and Tavern ; but fays nothing material happened there, during the three Weeks.

As it often happens for the wife and noble Pur-
pofes of Heaven, that one Misfortune fucceeds another, as clofe as the Waves on the Sea-fhore ; fo
the *Swallow* fet fail in Company with the *Vigilant*
Man of War, in Order to join the Admiral's Squadron ; and the next Night after their Departure, another violent Storm happened, in which
the *Swallow* not only loft fight of the *Vigilant*, but
alfo fprung her Main-maft, loft moft of her Rig-
ging, and was fo much damaged in her Hold, that
all the Sailors and Marines were obliged to take
their feveral Turns at the Pump, which is by far a
harder Piece of Labour, than thofe who have never
tried it are apt to imagine. Such a Series of Calamities fucceeding each other fo faft, and fo un-
expectedly

expectedly, were, in all Appearance, fufficient to
daunt the ftrongeft Refolution, and cool the Courage
of the braveft young Sailor that ever trod the Deck
of a Ship. But fome Minds are caft, if I may fo
fpeak, in fo happy a Mould, that Danger and Difficulties inftead of depreffing, raife them above
themfelves, enlarge their Views, and animate them
to ftem the Tide of Adverfity, which they rarely
fail to furmount by Steadinefs and Perfeverance.
To this favourite Clafs of Mortals our Heroine belonged, fince on this Occafion fhe not only willingly took her Turn at the Pump of a finking
Veffel, but alfo performed the feveral Offices of
a common Sailor, and in both Qualities behaved
with fuch Judgment and Intrepidity, that, next
under God, fhe was looked upon by the Ship's
Company as a Kind of Deliverer, and an Inftrument of their Prefervation. The *Swallow* after this
Difafter made the beft of her Way to *Gibraltar*,
were as foon as they arrived, fhe went on Shore,
and attended Lieutenaut *Richard Wigate*, Lieutenant of the Marines, who was very ill, and lodged
at Mrs. *Davis*'s on the Hill.

THE Ship refitted here with the utmoft Expedition, and failed for the *Madiera* Iflands, where
fhe took in fuch Wines, and other Provifions, as
was thought neceffary for the intended Voyage. As
Providence is always Kind to Diftrefs, fhe here met
with the *Sheernefs* Privateer of *Briftol*, whofe Commander generoufly fupplied her with a fufficient
Number of Hands, and from thence, they failed
to the Cape of *Good Hope*, and in their Voyage,
were put upon Short, and fome time after upon
Half Allowance.

DURING their Paffage, their Allowance was fhort-
ened, as I juft beforementioned, and that which
they had, was falt and bad, and befides there was fo
great a Scarcity of Water on board, that they were
                                              allow'd

allowed only a Pint a Day for some Time; all which, must have been great Hardships to her.

WHEN they arrived at the Cape, they there met with the Admiral in the *Namur*, which was great Joy to them; and our Heroine being disappointed hitherto of meeting her faithless Husband, and now seeing the Fleet all in Company, was in hopes of acquiring some Glory as a Soldier, knowing the Reason of this Fleet's being fitted out was to annoy the Enemies of her Country, which soon happened according to her Wishes, as the Fleet soon sailed from this Port for *Morusus*, on which Place they began their first Attack; and though unexperienced in the Use of Arms, except in learning her Exercise, she behaved with an uncommon Bravery, and exerted herself in her Country's Cause.

THIS Attack did not hold long; our brave Admiral finding this impracticable, and unwilling to lose his Ships and Men, for whom he had great Regard, left that Place, and sailed for Fort St. *David*'s, where they arrived in a little Time, and the Marines being put on Shore joined the *English* Army, and encamped, and in about three Weeks marched and encamped before *Elacapong*, and laid Siege to it, with an Intent to storm the Place. This fresh Adventure inspired her with fresh Hopes of shewing her undaunted Courage, which she did to the Admiration of her Officers; but on the tenth Day of the Siege, a Shell from the *English* took the Magazine of the Enemy, and blew it up, which occasioned them to surrender at Discretion.

I CANNOT help reflecting a little upon the Hardships, Fatigues and Dangers she incountered from the Time she left *Lisbon* in *Europe*, till her Arrival before *Pondicherry* in *Asia*, so many Vicissitudes, as were sufficient to damp the Spirits of an *Alexander* or a *Cæsar*, Storms, Hurricanes and
pinching

pinching Want, were her Concomitants, pumping
an almoſt wrecked Veſſel, was her moſt conſtant
(tho' laborious) Employment ; ſeventeen Weeks
ſhort Allowance from the *Maderas* to the *Cape* of
Good Hope, was all ſhe had to ſubſiſt upon ;
Attacks upon fortified Towns, ſome of which
were impregnable, where Bomb-Shells and Can-
nons were inceſſantly diſplaying Death where-
ever they fell; at other Times, moving, marching,
and encamping ; I ſay ſuch Reflections and gloomy
Proſpects, prove the Cauſe of many ſuch Hard-
ſhips and Difficulties even in the moſt robuſt of the
Maſculine Gender, how much more in one of the
tender Sex, who are afraid of Shaddows, and ſhud-
ders at the Preſſage of a Dream.

I SHALL now proceed to their March to *Pondicherry*, which is but a few Leagues from the forementioned Place; they encamped within about
three Miles from the Town, *Boſcawen* being then
both Admiral and General, and Major *Mount Plea-
ſant* informed them with their Intention, which
was to ſtorm the Place, which Attack was began by
the Ships firing at the Fort, ſome of which Time
they lay Middle-deep in Water in their Trenches :
This Attack continued eleven Weeks, part of which
Time they had no Bread, moſt of their Food
being Rice ; and the many Bombs and Shells
thrown among them, killed and wounded many of
their Men. During this Space of Time, ſhe behaved
with the greateſt Bravery and Intrepidity, ſuch as
was conſiſtent with the Character of an *Engliſh*
Soldier, and though ſo deep in Water, fired 37
Rounds of Shot, and received a Shot in the Groin,
ſix Shots in one Leg, and five in the other.

THE Siege being now broke up, by reaſon of
the heavy Rains, and violent Claps of Thunder,
it being the Time of the Year when the *Monzoons*
(for ſo they are called in that Country) happens,
The

she was sent to an Hospital at *Cuddalorom*, under the Care of two able Phyſicians, *viz*. Mr. *Belchier* and Mr. *Hancock*; but ſhe, not willing to be diſcovered, extracted the Ball out of her Groin herſelf, and always dreſt that Wound; and in about three Months was perfectly cured; but moſt of the Fleet being ſailed before her Recovery, ſhe was left behind, and ſent on board the *Tartar Pink*, which then lay in the Harbour, where ſhe remained, doing the Duty of a Sailor, till the Return of the Fleet from *Madraſs*, when ſhe was turned over to the *Eltham*, Captain *Lloyd* Commander, and ſailed for *Bombay*, where they arrived in about ten Days, being ſcarce of Hands, having only eight in a Watch, of which ſhe was one; and what made their Fatigue ſtill more, was their being obliged to keep continually at the Pump, the Ship having ſprung a Leak in her Larboard Bow.

At *Bombay* they were obliged to heave the Ship down in Order to clean her Bottom, which kept them there about five Weeks, and then they ſailed to *Monſerrat*, to take the *Royal Duke Indiaman* under Convoy, to bring her to Fort St. *David's*, where ſhe was gone for Proviſions.

At *Bombay* her Maſter being on Shore, ſhe was obliged to watch in her turn, as is uſual on ſuch Occaſions; but being one Night on Duty, Mr. *Allen*, who then had the Command of the Ship, being on Shore, deſired her to ſing for him, which ſhe begged that he would excuſe, as ſhe was not very well; but he being proud in this his new Employ, as Commander, abſolutely commanded her to ſing; which ſhe refuſed to do, as ſhe did not think it any incumbent Duty for a Soldier to ſing when commanded ſo to do, and that by one who was not an Officer in their Core, or had ſhe any Obligations to him; however this Refuſal proved of fatal Conſequence to her; he ordered her immediately into

Irons,

Irons, which accordingly was done, and continued for the Space of five Days, and then ordered her to have a dozen Lashes, which she had at the Gang-Way of the Ship, and after that sent to the Fore-top-maft-head, for four Hours; such is the Cruelty of those that are invested with Power, and do not know how to ufe it. However, this Man's Cruelty did not go unpunished; for after there Arival in *England*, as they were unriging the Ship, one of the Sailors let a Block fall on his Head, which hurt him greatly.

THEY now, with the *Royal Duke*, failed from *Montferrat* to Fort St. *David's*, and was there at the Time of the great Hurricane, when the *Namur* and *Pembroke*, and other Ships were loft: The *Eltham*, of which she was on board, had fome Share in the faid Hurricane, for she broke her Cables, and was forced to Sea; but happily returned in again to the Port without receiving any great Damage.

Now during her stay here at Fort St. *David's*, she had frequent Opportunities, and Caufes for Reflection: She went on Shore fundry Times along with fome of the Men, where her Ears and her Eyes were often affected with the difagreeable Sound of horrible Oaths, and many lewd Actions and Geftures, fuch as ftripping themfelves naked, when they went to fwim, a Sight, which however difagreeable it might appear to her, yet she was forced to make a Virtue of Necessity, by openly conforming herfelf to thofe rude, indifcreet, and unwomanly Actions, which she filently diffavoured and contemned. But here the unpolished Tars had not Opportunities of extending their Wickednefs to fuch a high Pitch as they would have done, had they had Objects to fatiate their brutish Appetites; for there were but a few white Women in the Place; however she faw too much not to be affected, left her Sex should by their impudent, and un-

- D   limited

limited Behaviour, be difcovered, and her Virtue
facrificed to their rapacious, boundlefs and luftful
Appetites ; but Innocency and Virtue is the fafeft
Protection in the worft of Times ; and this was
what fheltered her from the much dreaded Calamity
that threatned her.

On the 19th of *November* laft, the *Eltham* failed
with the reft of the Fleet from Fort St. *David's*,
and kept Company till they came to the Cape of
Good Hope ; when the *Eltham* had Orders to make
the beft of her Way to *Lisbon*, to take in Money for
the Ufe of the Merchants of *London*.

The Day after they left Fort St. *David's*, her
Mafter Lieutenant *Wyegate* died, in whofe Death
fhe loft the only Friend fhe had on board, and
where to find fuch another, fhe knew not : This
brought afrefh into her Mind the Remembrance
of her faithlefs Hufband, whofe Villainy and Cruelty had drove her to all the Straits, Hardfhips and
Dangers fhe endured both by Sea and Land, and had
reduced her to the wretched State fhe was then in.
Thefe Reflections were fufficient to have funk the
Spirits of the moft hardy Hero ; but fhe bore them
with a becoming Refignation. She was diftinguifhed
amongft the Ship's Crew for her Ingenuity in wafh-
ing and mending of Linnen, but as it is common on board of King's Ships to have fome Men
who are dexterous at fuch Performances, fhe was
not fufpected upon that Score.

Some Time after the Death of Lieutenant *Wyegate*, fhe was taken into the Service of Lieutenant
Kite, fecond Lieutenant of the Ship, and continued fo about two Months ; when he getting a Boy,
he recommended her to Mr. *Wallace*, third Lieutenant of the Ship, who proved alfo a very good
Mafter to her. But now fhe was laid open (though
contrary to her Inclination) to the Company of the
Sailors,

Sailors, for they were used, when she had her Head shaved, to enquire why she did not shave her Beard; her Answer was, that she was too young. Upon which they used to damn her, calling her Miss *Molly Gray*, she used to return the uncivil Compliment, by damning them, and telling them, that she could prove herself, as she had always done, during the Voyage, as good a Man as any Seaman on board, and that she would lay them a Wager upon that Point.

DURING this long Voyage, they often used, as I have just said, on account of her smooth Face, to burlesque her, by swearing she was a Woman. This Expression, however indifferently they meant it, gave her abundance of Trouble; she fore-saw what the Consequence would be, in case this Joke was carried too far; to prevent which, she with a masculine but modest Assurance, told them, that if they would lay any Wager, she would give them ocular Demonstration of her being as much a Man as the best in the Ship; which Reply had the desired Effect, seeing it put a Stop to their further Suggestions: Next, they began to declare her to be a Woman on account of her smooth Face, seeing she had no Beard; but she told them that she was so very young, that it could not be supposed she should have a Beard so soon; however, she could not prevent their calling her by the Name of *Molly Gray*, which Appellation she went by during the Voyage, until they arrived at *Lisbon*.

WHILE they lay at *Lisbon*, she often went on Shore in Company with the Ships Crew, upon Parties of Pleasure, and was always their Companion in their Revellings; this Part she acted, not out of Choice, but for wise Ends. She remember'd in what Manner she had been reflected upon by them during the Voyage from St. *David's* to *Lisbon*, therefore she pointed out this Method as the most

D 2   effectual,

effectual, to prevent any further suspicious *Reflections for the future.* She very wisely judged, that by associating herself with them, by shewing a free and chearful Disposition, and by being ready to come into their Measures, she should banish from their Imaginations the least Suspicion of her being a Woman, and by that Means enjoy a free and uninterrupted Passage to her native Country, without discovering her Sex. There was one of the Ship's Crew, named *Edward Jefferies*, an intimate Acquaintance, a Marine, and Mess-mate of her's; they two had contracted an Acquaintance and Familiarity with two young Women in *Lisbon*, the handsomest of which was the favourite of our Heroine; but *Jefferies* taking a greater liking to her Choice than his own, proposed to toss up who should have her, which she readily agreed to, not caring how soon she should be rid of such a Companion: This *Jefferies* on tossing up gained the Lady, upon which she readily resigned her into his Hands, and made that serve as a good Excuse for being rid of them both. This Intimacy subsisted between them and the *Portugueze* Women while they remained at *Lisbon*, and when they were about to set sail for *England*, their Sweethearts came to the Ship's side in order to take Leave of them, but was prevented from coming on board, by the Command of the Captain.

We shall leave the candid Reader at liberty to judge the Disorders, Terrors and Distractions that so many various Scenes must have plunged her into; such a Disquiet, that she had not felt the like in all her past Enterprizes. A thousand Inquietudes rolled in upon her, like so many Billows, and almost sunk her down into the Abyss of Despair. She began to reflect upon the many Vicissitudes she had underwent, since her first launching out into the boisterous Sea of War, occasioned by the Cruelty of a perfidious Husband. What Dangers, what Hardships,

fhips, and what Fatigues fhe had underwent! The many Inconveniences fhe had overcome, and the Difficulties fhe had furmounted, in preferving her Virtue untainted in the midft of fo many vicious and prophane Actions, as had often been reprefented in their blackeft Sable to her view, and that fhe had hitherto come off Conquerefs, and when almoft at the Door of her native Country, unfullied and undefiled by any of thefe Temptations wherewith fhe had been affaulted; then to be in the greateft Danger; then to have that Virtue, which had hitherto been her affiftant and comfortable Companion in all her adverfe Fortune, tore from her Breaft, and nothing left behind but Shame, Guilt and Confufion. Thefe Reflections had almoft vanquifhed her great Spirit, had not her good Genius led her to put in Practice the Scheme fhe had formed at *Lisbon*, which anfwered the End fhe aimed at, and by which her Virtue, which was always dear to her, remains ftill untainted, to her immortal Praife.

On the Affair of the Supply of the Men they had from the *Sheernefs* Privateer at *Madeira*, fhe gave the following Account; which was, that after they were come on board the *Swallow* Sloop, fome of them feemed very penfive; fo that her Curiofity led her to enquire into the Reafon of their Grief, which fhe found was occafioned by their being brought on board a Man of War, which at firft to her feemed ftrange, not being acquainted with the Manner of Men being impreffed; and having often converfed with fome of them, found they were fent on board by Force; and fome of them having Wives and Children in *England*, and fome in *Ireland*, the Thoughts of their long Separation from their Wives and Families, and the uncertainty of ever feeing them again, was the chief Caufe of their Sorrows.

THIS

THIS Relation, and the Anxieties fome of them fhewed, gave her new Matter of Contemplation, and often, when retired in her Mafter's Cabin, reflected on her own Fate, having herfelf been married to a moft faithlefs Man, who had left her in the utmoft Diftrefs, at a Time fhe was not able to help herfelf, and that without any Reafon, but what was occafioned by his own Extravagances. But here fhe found the Difference in that Sex, and that greater then fhe ever conceived before: Here fhe faw Men in the greateft Affliction, for being forced from them they loved ; offering there all for Liberty to return to their native Land and Families, whilft her perfideous Hufband's chief Care was to avoid her. However, it was fome Confolation to her, in thefe her diftreffed Circumftances, to find fome on board, and who fhe concluded muft be her Companions as Shipmates, infpired with Sentiments of Honour and Virtue ; fhe alfo reflected on the unhappy Circumftances of thofe poor Women and Children thefe Men had left behind, and often wifhed fhe could have an Opportunity of relating to them what fhe now faw ; imagining from her own Cafe, that it would be fome Confolation to them to hear fo great Proof of their Affections. She at firft blamed them for going to Sea on board the Privateer, but when fhe was informed that it was only for a little Time, and they not bound to ferve longer, than a certain Time fpecified in their Articles, and that their chief Motives was to ferve their Families ; in fo doing fhe looked on them as real Objects of Compaffion, which occafioned her to fympathize with them ; and though Fortune had been fo unkind to herfelf, fhe could not refrain thinking of theirs, and often endeavoured to affwage their Sorrows, by recommending to them Hopes of a happy Return to *England* ; and alfo procured every Thing which fhe thought neceffary for them on board, which was fomewhat in her Power, hav-

ing

ing Recourfe to all her Mafter's Stores, efpecially his
Liquors, which was pretty plentiful at that Time.

I SHALL depart a little from the Subject, and
give the Reader an Account of that bafeft of Men,
our Heroine's Husband, who upon deferting his
lawful Wife, entered himfelf as a Foremaft Man
on board one of his Countrymen, then lying in the
River *Thames.* But where can the guilty Criminal
fly for Sanctuary ? His own Confcience muft prove
his Executioner, and a thoufand Monitors within,
who Vulture like, always gnaw the Liver, not
fuffering the Mind to enjoy the fhorteft Interval of
Quiet ; this admirable Truth has been fully verified
in him, according to the moft fubftantial Circumftances, as fhall hereafter be made appear.

ONE Day at *Lisbon,* on her Return to *Eugland,*
falling in Company with many of her Ship-mates,
they all went into an *Irifh* Houfe, by the *Ramanado's,*
to drink fome Wine, where was fitting at the fame
Time an *Englifhman,* a Sailor, who had lately
come from *Genoa* on board a *Dutch* Veffel ; there
were fome of his Brother Tars in Company who
knew him ; upon which they became very merry,
and began, over their Glafs and their Pipe, to
talk over fome of their Adventures, and what they
met with in their Travels worthy taking Notice
of ; and fhe, acoording to her conftant Practice,
was enquiring amongft the Mariners if any of them
knew one *James Summs,* who, fhe faid, had formerly been an intimate Acquaintance of her's ;
upon which this Stranger broke Speech, and told 'em
of an Affair that happened at *Genoa* while he was
there. There was, fays he, a *Dutchman* of that
Name, a Sailor, imprifoned there, for ftabbing a
Native of the Place, a Perfon of fome Diftinction,
with a Knife, of which Wound he foon expired ;
I, with two or three more of our Countrymen ap-
pointed to go and vifit him under this his Misfortune,

tune, which we accordingly did : When we came
to the Place, we were introduced by a Kind of
Officer, where he lay in a melancholy Situation ;
but upon our entering the Room, he raised himself
up from the Place where he had reclined his Head,
and saluted us in *English* ; then we began to con-
dole his Misfortune: Upon which, finding us affected with his melancholy Situation, and the cruel
Punishment he was about to suffer, he spoke to us
in the following Manner. Gentlemen, The Crime
I am to die for I committed, therefore my Punishment will be just whenever it falls : But this is not
the only Crime I stand indicted for at the Bar of
that All-seeing Judge, who searches into the inner-
most Recesses of our most concealed Actions, and
who pursues the Guilty where-ever they go; I,
who am here condemned for Murder, a few Years
ago lived in *Wapping*, *London*, my Name is *James
Summs*, a *Dutchman* by Birth; I married a young
Woman there, named *Hannah Snell*, born in *Worcester*, but who then lodged with a Brother-in-
Law, a Carpenter in *Ship-street:* We had not
been long joined in Matrimony before she proved
with Child; and I, forgetting my Duty as a Husband, and an approaching Father, gave a loose to
my vicious Inclinations, eloped from the Partner of
my Bed, and the one half of myself, went and
took up my Residence amongst a Parcel of lewd,
base Women, who withdrew my Affections entirely from her, who had the only just Title to it ;
and to satisfy their insatiable and extravagant Demands, I drained her of her all. This proved only
the Downfall to my future Calamities ; for my
Substance being now exhausted, thrust out of Doors
by these *Ladies of Pleasure*, who proved to me *Ladies of Pain*, and being ashamed to look my much
injured Wife in the Face any more, whom I had
so basely betrayed, my Mind was rack'd with ex-
quisite Torture, so that I would willingly have fled
from myself if it had been possible. A thousand
Inven-

Inventions came into my Head how I fhould difpofe of myfelf at this critical Juncture. I employed all the Skill I was mafter of to be affifting
in extricating me out of this Dilemma; at laft I
refolved to go on board one Ship or other, in order
to make a Voyage.

THE firft Ship I boarded was a *Rotterdam* Trader,
who accepted me in the Capacity of a Sailor, having but few Hands, the Steerfman agreed to give
me 40 Guilders *per* Month. A few Days afterwards we made down with the Tide, and failed
over to *Rotterdam*, where we unloaded: We had
not been many Days here, before an unforefeen
Accident happened, which was like to have produced fatal Confequences: One of the Boys going
one Day into the Steerage with a lighted Candle,
where was fome Powder loofe; a Spark from the
Candle dropt into the Powder, which in an Inftant
blew up, and did great Damage to the Veffel. This
Accident was charged upon me by two of the
Men who bore me a Grudge; upon which I was
Keel-haul'd, and received many Lafhes befides.
This ill Ufage provoked me much, fo that I de-
termined to quit my Mafter's Service, and let him
know that I intended to leave him; upon which he
paid me my Wages, and we parted. I then entered myfelf on board an *Irifh* Merchant, bound to
Lisbon, which Voyage I performed, and returned to
Cork, the Place where the Cargo was to be dif-
pofed of.

HERE, after I had received my Wages, I was
difcharged, and falling into bad Company, my
Wages was foon fpent, and being without Money,
Cloaths or Friends, in a ftrange Country, made my
Cafe very deplorable, which brought into my
Mind, my wicked Proceedings to my dear Wife,
and I lookt upon thofe Afflictions I underwent, as a
juft Punifhment from Heaven, for my wicked

E   Actions;

Actions; however, these Reflections soon gave
Way to Self-preservation; I was in great Diftrefs,
and how to work my Deliverance, was the main
Subject of my Thoughts; at the very fame Time,
there was a *Portuguefe* Veffel lying in the Harbour,
bound to *Genoa*; they wanted a few Hands, fome
of their own Men having died in the Voyage; I
proffered my Service, they accepted of me, ftaid in
Cork, a few Days afterwards, then weighed Anchor,
and fet fail for *Genoa*, where we arrived in Safety
in about three Weeks; here we had not continued
long, before I perpetrated the Murther, for which
I am about to fuffer: Now Gentlemen, I have
given you a full Account of the moft material Incidents that has happened to me fince I left *England*,
I therefore earneftly intreat the Favour of you,
when once you return to *England*, to enquire after my Wife, and if you find her, be pleafed in
my Name, to prefent her the Love of a dying
Hufband, who confcious of his Guilt, humbly
begs her Pardon and Forgivenefs, for all the Inju-
ries he hath done her, fince firft he knew her; this
his Requeft we promifed to fulfil, if once we returned to *England*; fo we took our laft Farewel.
None of us, ever faw him afterwards, but were
informed, that he was fewed up in a Sack, with
heavy Stones, and thrown into the Sea; the other
two *Englifhmen* failed for *Leghorn*, and I for this
Place, and when I go Home, I intend to make an
Enquiry concerning the faid Woman: She liftened
attentively all the While he was relating this Story,
and weighing all the particular Circumftances of
this Relation, fhe perceived fo many concurring
Circumftances blended together, as put it beyond
all Doubt he was her Hufband; this Account however, notwithftanding his vile Proceedings, grieved
her much, and no doubt would have broke forth
into briny Tears, had fhe been in a Place of Re-
tirement: She fometimes grieved at his cruel and
untimely Fate, but fuddenly, the ill Treatment fhe

met

met with from him, returned triumphant in her
Mind, and extinguished her kindled Tenderness:
However, she told the Sailor who related this Story,
that from the Account he gave of this Man, he
must have been the same identical Person, with
whom she had formerly been acquainted, and if
once she came to *England*, she would endeavour to
find out the Wife of this unfortunate Man, whom
she knew very well, and would acquaint her with
this Catastrophe, and by so saying, concealed herself entirely from the least Suspicion.

Having now finished the Account of her Hus-
bands untimely End, as related to her at *Lisbon* ;
the Detail of which, appeared to her, as if sent
from above, to free her from those anxious Cares,
which, in the midst of the greatest Dangers, always set triumphant in her Breast, I shall now proceed to her Voyage from thence to *England*.

They set sail from *Lisbon* the 3d of *May*, and
arrived at *Spithead* the 1st of *June*, without any
Thing material during the Voyage (which was
lengthened by Calms and contrary Winds) ; that
very Day she arrived at *Spithead* she came on Shore,
and took a Lodging along with several of her Shipmates and Marines, at one *James Cunningham's*, at
the Sign of the *Jolly Marine* and *Sailor*; where the
House being thronged with Lodgers, she was o-
bliged to be Bedfellow to one *John Huchins*, a
Brother Marine, the first Night ; but during her
short Stay in *Portsmouth*, in her often Rovings in
and about the Town, (which was only two Days
and three Nights) she happen'd to meet with the
Sister of Mr. *Cunningham*, the Drum-Major's Wife,
one *Catherine* ———, with whom she had cultivated a
slender Acquaintance at the Time she first enlisted there. This young Woman knew *Hannah*
to be the young Soldier that had enlisted and been

sent

fent abroad with Admiral *Bofcowen*, and expreffed fome Joy at her fafe Return: Then entering into this Converfation, introduced a farther Intimacy; and *Hannah*, rather than fit to drink with her Shipmates, fpent moft of her Time with this young Woman. This Opportunity improved their Converfation, and fometimes they converfed upon Love; and *Hannah* finding this young Woman had no diflike to her, fhe endeavoured to try if fhe could not act the Lover as well as the Soldier, which fhe fo well effected, that it was agreed upon fhe fhould return from *London*, in order to be married as foon as fhe had got her Difcharge and Pay; and tho' but fo fhort a Time there as two Days, had effected this her Amour fo as to obtain the young Woman's Confent to marry her.

In order to countenance this her Scheme, fhe told the fuppofed Object of her Love, that as foon as fhe arrived at *London*, and received her Wages, fhe would remit the fame to her; and when fhe had vifited, and tarried fome time with each of her nigh Relations and intimate Friends, fhe would then return to *Portfmouth*, according to Agreement, and confummate their matrimonial Ceremonies with a Solemnity fuitable to her Abilities.

THE next Night, being *Saturday* the 2d of *June*, *Hannah's* Bedfellow, who had lain with her the Night before, went out of Town, and one *James Moody*, who had been a Ship-mate with her on board the *Eltham* from Fort St. *David's* to *England*, coming in the Evening of that Day, and wanting a Lodging, he was received by the Landlord, and as *Hannah* was his intimate, he was admitted to be her Bedfellow, which continued for two Nights together, without the leaft Sufpicion in Life.

MY

It is here worthy of Observation, that this Woman should lay three Nights with two different Men, one of whom who had been her Companion and Fellow-adventurer, during the Space of fifteen Months and more; and never, during that Space of Time, discover the least Hint of her being of the female Kind; and this Man had often been her Assistant in the most dangerous Exploits, and could not avoid acknowledging, that she behaved upon all Occasions, with the greatest Bravery and Resolution.

Whitmonday, being the 4th of *June*, she set out from *Portsmouth* for *London*; accompanied by *George Orley*, a Serjeant of Marines, who was a Partner with her in her Adventures, and who, together with nine Marines, accompanied her to *London*: She received before they set out from *Portsmouth*, five Shillings Conduct-money. The first Place she traveled to after her Departure from *Portsmouth*, was *Petersfield*, in *Hampshire*; where she lay all Night, with one *Andrew Gray*, a Marine, not only in the same Regiment, but in the same Company: Next Day travel'd as far as *Guildford*, where the aforesaid *Andrew Gray* and she were Bedfellows; next Night she arrived in *London*, where she disingaged herself from her old Intimates, and lodged along with her Brother, Mr. *James Gray*, Carpenter, in *Ship-Street*, *Wapping*; where she now resides.

Now I have brought my female Adventurer home again to her native Country, after near five Years Adventures; prompted thereto by the ill Usage of a faithless Husband, who, after first stripping her of her all, and then eloping, prompted her to the Resolution of disguising herself, by putting on Men's Apparel, going into the Country without the Knowledge of her Brother, Sister, or any other of her Friends, in search of him who had

thus

thus abufed her; and entering into Colonel *Guife's* Regiment of Foot, then lying at *Coventry*, who from thence marched to *Carlifle*, where fhe was ill ufed, the Particulars of which, are fet forth at large in the foregoing Pages: How fhe received five hundred Lafhes at *Carlifle*, as a Punifhment for her virtuous Conduct; her 'Refolution' to defert; and her puting this Determination into Execution; her changing her military Cloathing about a Mile from Town, for the ruftick Garb of a Shepherd; her Arrival at *Portfmouth*; her entering into General *Frafer's* Regiment of Marines, her being draughted out for the *Eaft Indies*; her embarking on board the *Swallow* Sloop of War, under the Command of Admiral *Bofcowen*, and the many Viciffitudes fhe underwent during the Series of her Adventures, until her fafe (though unexpected) return to her Native Country, where, after her Arrival, fhe met with fundry humorous Incidents; with many other material Circumftances, the Particulars of which is here fet down at large; but not to fwell this Treatife with any Thing fictitious or doubtful, I have afferted nothing but plain Matter of Fact as here fet down.

I would have my candid Readers furvey in Imagination, the many various Scenes that here difplay themfelves with a moft furprizing Luftre. Here is a Woman, and an *Englifh* Woman, who, notwithftanding the many Dangers and Viciffitudes fhe underwent for near the Space of five Years, during her Travels, was never found out to be of the feminine Gender. It is true many threatned Difcoveries were attempted by her Shipmates and Fellow-Adventurers, which derived its Influence from her not having a Beard; but her ready Turns of Mind undeceived all thofe who fhewed themfelves overbufy in prying into this Secret: This her Conduct, very furprizingly preferved her Virtue from becoming a Sacrifice to the Impetuofity of the carnal Defires of both her

Superiors

Superiors and Inferiors ; for can it be imagined, that in the midst of so many Dangers, where there was no Back-Door to creep out at, if her Sex had been discovered, but she must have fallen a Victim to the loose, disorderly, and vitious Appetites of many on board, especially those whom she was more immediately concerned with, to wit, her Officers. These Reflections must possess the Reader with generous Sentiments of this our Heroine, who by her Subtilty, and ready Inventions, destroyed in the Embrio, every Thing advanced by her Fellow-Shipmates, that she imagined might be a Means of exposing her Virtue.

Such an Adventure as this, is not to be met with in the Records of either antient or modern Observations, therefore, for the Sake of the *British* Nation, ought to be recorded in Golden Characters on a Statue of Marble for succeeding Ages, to peruse with Admiration, that an *English* Woman should, *Amazon* like, not only enter herself upon the List in behalf of her Country at Home, but boldly and resolutely launch out into the most remote Corners of the Earth, upon enterprizing and dangerous Adventures, the like never attempted before by any of her Sex, even daring Fate, as it were, to execute his most rigorous Inflictions upon her ; the many Strugglings and Conflicts she encounter'd during the Course of her Travels, not being used to the watery Element, and the many Revolutions that often happen upon the Surface of the Deep ; the many Duties she was obliged to execute, in the midst of Hundreds of the most unpolite Part of Mankind, such as Tars ; the many Fears and Suspicions she harboured least her Sex should be discovered, to avoid which, she proved her own Physician, in extracting the Ball out of her Wound, to prevent that Discovery which must unavoidably have happened, had she permitted the Surgeons to have performed their regular Operations: These, with many more, (seemingly

ingly infurmountable Difficulties) did this our *Bri-tifb* Heroine undergo, and overcome, by her fafe Arrival in her native Country, as before-mentioned.

WHEN fhe arrived in *London*, fhe went to her Brother in Law's Houfe, in *Ship-Street, Wapping;* where he lived at the Time when fhe went abroad ; fhe no fooner entered the Houfe, than her Sifter (notwithftanding her Difguife) knew her, but her Brother in Law, Mr. *Gray* being in Bed, fhe went to his Bedfide, being defirous to fee him, where he lay in a Slumber, and embraced him, upon which he awoke, and feeing a Perfon in a Soldier's Drefs, coming to his Bedfide in fuch a Manner and imbracing him, furprifed him much, however, he was foon freed from this Surprize by her difcovering herfelf, which afforded him a great deal of Satisfaction ; as fhe was his great Favourite before fhe went abroad, and her fudden and unexpected Appearance, caufed a great deal of Joy, in the whole Family ; after refrefhing herfelf with a Part of what the Houfe afforded, fhe diverted her Brother and Sifter 'till Bed-time, with fome Part of her Adventures, which relation forced Tears from their Eyes.

THERE was at this Time a Female Lodger in Mr. *Gray*'s Houfe, of whom Mr. *Gray* requefted, that fhe would admit a Sifter of his for a Bedfellow, to which fhe readily agreed : But when the Sifter was introduced, the young Woman, who was then in Bed, was very much furprized to fee a Soldier fit down to undrefs himfelf in her Bed-Chamber ; but Mr. *Gray* and his Wife difcovered the Secret, which, notwithftanding, fhe would not Credit, until fhe had occular Demonftration. This was the firft, next to her Brother and Sifter, that fhe difcovered herfelf to, and ever fince they have been Bedfellows, which made the Neighbours report (imagining her to be a Man) that the young Woman was married to a Soldier, and this great Untruth was reported for Fact throughout the whole Neighbourhood.

SOMETIME after this, she, in Company with her Sister and suppofed Wife, went to *Weftminfter*, in order to fee her Friends, who were very much diffatisfy'd at her carrying a ftrange Woman in Company with her fuppofed Brother, who perhaps, upon receiving his Money, might decoy him into fome Place of bad Fame, where he might chance to lofe it all in an Inftant. This, together with fome former Paffages, conftrains me to obferve how much the Publick, both at Home and Abroad, have been deceived in this Woman, fhe being fo long in the Army and Navy, where there were many penetrating clear-fighted Gentlemen, and afhore in foreign Countries amongft Men, Women and Children; and notwithftanding all thefe publick Characters, her Sex not difcovered. This muft caufe Admiration in every Reader; but fhe counterfeited the Man fo dextroufly, and does to this very Day, that the moft excellent Judge of Features, Semetry or Gefture, cannot difcover the Deceit.

BUT that I may not fuffer any of my inquifitive Readers to remain in fufpence concerning fome particular Adventures that befel her, the bare Relation of which may not be altogether fo fatisfactory, I fhall explain thofe which appear moft Paradoxical, in order not only to fatisfy every Reader, but alfo to prevent any future Reflections that might occafionally arife from fuch a Neglect.

WHEN fhe firft enter'd into the Service at *Coventry*, fhe marched to *Carlifle*, where fhe was Whipt for Neglect of Duty, being unjuftly accufed by Serjeant *Davis*, as is fully mentioned in the

the preceding Pages. The Method she used to prevent the Discovery of her Sex was this, according to her own Declaration : Her Breasts were then not so big by much as they are at present, her Arms being extended and fixed to the City Gates, her Breasts were drawn up, and consequently did not appear so large ; and besides this, her Breast was to the Wall, and could not be discovered by any of her Comrades ; and when she was Whipt on board, her Hands being lashed to the Gangway, she stood upright, and tied a Handkerchief round her Neck, to prevent, as it were, any Lashes that she might accidentally receive there, to conceal her Breasts, which were covered by the Ends of the Handkerchief falling over them, and thereby prevented a Discovery which must unavoidably have happened, had not she thus acted. And what the Consequences of such an unravell'd Secret would have produced, she was at a Loss to imagine, the Thoughts of which perplexed her incessantly ; however, she escaped being discovered at this Juncture also, as well as at many more, when she imagined herself in the most imminent Dangers : But all those adverse Turns gave an Edge to her Inventions, and by that means extricated her out of the many Difficulties she was involved in.

THIS the Reader may plainly perceive throughout the whole Narration ; and I am convinced, that no Age or Country, ever produced a more distinguished Instance of Virtue, Conduct and Resolution, than is to be met with in this our Heroine's Adventures, which is worthy to be transmitted to latest Posterity ; to inform succeeding Ages, that such an Instance of Heroism was not to be found in the *British* Annals, that the like could not be met with, in the Observations of any Nation in the World, that a Woman, whose mould is tender, delicate and unable to endure Fatigues, and who is terrified at the Name of Dangers, should under-

go

go fo many Scenes without relinquifhing her Refolution of keeping her Sex a Secret.

I HAD forgot to mention a Circumftance worthy of Notice, in its proper Place, which happened at *Lisbon*, concerning the two Sweethearts, fhe and *Edward Jefferies* had there, as is before mentioned; which was, that when fhe and *Jefferies* were on board before they fet fail from *Lisbon* to *England*, thefe two young Women, of whom mention is made, came along the Ship's Side in a Boat, and called for *James Gray*, and fhe being informed thereof, went into the Boat where they were, but after a little Converfation, fhe found them inclined to come on board, and remain there while they lay in the River; fhe promifed to afk Leave of the Captain for their Reception, but a frefh and feafonable Thought came into her Head, which was, that if they came on board, and continued any Time, they might fooner difcover her than any of the Men, therefore to prevent the worft, inftead of pleading for their Admittance, fhe requefted of the Captain, that they fhould not be fuffered to come on board. This Requeft was not only intended for her own Prefervation, but likewife to preferve the Women from being debauched by the Sailors, which they could not have avoided, had they came on board; by which Means, both fhe and they efcaped the threatned Danger.

I KNOW the Reader will be defirous to know how the Ball was extracted out of her Groin, and will imagine, that it was next to an Impoffibility it could be performed without a Difcovery. Now to rectify the Scruples of fuch, I fhall relate this Account as attefted by herfelf; which fhe faid was, that after fhe received the twelve Wounds, as before mentioned, fhe remained all that Day, and the following Night in the Camp, before fhe was carried to the Hofpital, and after fhe was brought there, and laid in a Kit, she continued till next Day in the greatest Agony and Pain, the Ball still remaining in the Flesh of that Wound in her Groin, and how to extract it she knew not, for she had not discovered to the Surgeons that she had any other Wound than those in her Legs. This Wound being so extreme painful, it almost drove her to the Precipice of Despair; she often thought of discovering herself, that by that Means she might be freed from the unspeakable Pain she endured, by having the Ball taken out by one of the Surgeons; but that Resolution was soon banished, and she resolved to run all Risques, even at the hazard of her Life, rather than that her Sex should be known. Confirmed in this Resolution, she communicated her Design to a black Woman, who attended upon her, and could get at the Surgeons Medicines, and desired her Assistance; and her Pain being so very great, that she was unable to endure it much longer, she intended to try an Experiment upon herself, which was, to endeavour to extract the Ball out of that Wound; but notwithstanding she discovered her Pain and Resolution to this Black, yet she did not let her know that she was a Woman. The Black readily came, and afforded her all the Assistance she could, by bringing her Lint and Salve to dress the Wound with, which she had recourse to, it being left in the Wards where the Patients lay; for which Act of Friendship she made her a Present of a Rupee at her Departure, which is 3 s. 4 d. of the Currency of that Country, but here in *England* it goes for no more than 2 s. 6 d. Now the Manner in which she extracted the Ball was full hardy and desperate: She prob'd the Wound with her Finger till she came where the Ball lay, and then upon feeling it, thrust in both her Finger and Thumb, and pulled it out. This was a very rough Way of proceeding with ones own Flesh; but of two Evils, as she thought, this was the least, so rather chusing to have her Flesh

tore

tore and mangled than her Sex difcovered. After this Operation was performed, fhe applied fome of the healing Salves which the Black had brought her, by the help of which fhe made a perfect Cure of that dangerous Wound.

THE Reader will here obferve, the invincible Courage and Refolution of this Woman, who in the midft of fo many Inconveniences as fhe daily encounter'd, fhould ftill be able to guard herfelf from a difcovery of her Sex ; but indeed it appears fhe acted fo artfully on every Emergency, as rendered any Attempts of this Kind abortive; for notwithftanding the Wound fhe received in her Groin was the moft dangerous of all the others, yet that was the only Wound fhe kept from the Knowledge of the Surgeons, by telling them, when they came to examine her, that all the Wounds fhe had received were in her Legs, which they readily believed ; and by that Means prevented any farther Search.

OBSERVE here the Steadinefs and Intrepidity wherewith fhe overcame all the Pains and Dangers which affaulted her. Who would not in the midft of fo much Agony and Pain as fhe felt here, broke through the ftrongeft and moft virtuous Refolutions in order to obtain immediate Relief ? But fhe remained ftill inflexible in the midft of every Affliction wherewith fhe was environed, no Confideration could ever prevail upon her in her own Mind to deviate from the Refolutions fhe had imbibed upon her firft Launching out, and which, though it coft her many a painful Hour, yet by her fteady Adherence to thefe Principles, fhe obtained a Conqueft over near five Years adverfe Fortune.

Now having fatisfied the Reader's Doubts in Regard to the Methods fhe ufed to conceal her Sex from the Knowledge of any about her, on thefe
particular

particular Occasions, when she was most exposed, *viz.* the twice she was whipt, and upon the dressing of her Wounds, which were Times I say, when Danger was at the Door ready to burst in, and plunder the Habitation of its most valuable Furniture; I shall next proceed, to shew the Reader some Transactions that has occur'd since she came to *London.*

Tho' she had not discovered her Sex to any besides her Brother in Law, her Sister, and the young Woman with whom she lodged ; she was very uneasy, fearing, lest a further Discovery should be made, and she thereby deprived of her Soldier's Pay. This Motive induced her to conceal herself as much as possible, till she had received her Pay, (being 15 Pounds) which she accordingly did on the *Saturday* after her Arrival in *London,* being the 9th Day of *June,* when she, with Serjeant *Orley,* *John Hutchins,* *James Moody,* *Andrew Grey,* and the rest of the Marines that came to *London* with her, went to the Agent *John Winter,* Esq; in *Downing-Street, Westminster* ; where being all paid and discharged, they went to an Alehouse, the Fighting-Cocks, next Door to Mr. *Winter*'s House, and there she first discovered herself to her Comrades. There being two Suits of Cloathing due to her from the Regiment, she also sold them for 16 s. being glad to get hold of all the Money she could before her Sex was discovered.

Now upon receiving her Pay, and all her fellow Adventures then present, she thought that was the most proper Opportunity she ever could have, for disclosing her Sex, seeing they could then testify the Truth of all the Fatigues, Dangers and other Incidents of her Adventures, and that her Sex was never discovered, which if then omitted, she might never have an Opportunity of seeing them all together again, and by that Means, the Account of her Adventures as aforesaid, might be lookt up-

on

on by the Publick as fictitious: Thefe Confidera-
tions prevailed upon her to embrace the then feafonable Occafion, for difcovering herfelf, before
they took a final Leave; fhe therefore propofed to
them to make merry before they parted, which was
agreed to by one and all of them, as they expected
never to meet altogether any more; and then fhe
difcovered herfelf to the whole Company which
caufed a univerfal Surprife amongft them all.

But after they had recovered themfelves from
this fudden Emotion, which the aforefaid furprizing
Information had thrown them into, they could
hardly be prevailed upon to believe the Truth of
what fhe advanced, until her Brother and Sifter undeceived them, by informing them of the whole
Tranfaction. Upon which, they all with one
Voice founded forth her Praife, by applauding her
Courage as a Soldier, her Dexterity as a Sailor, her
humane Deportment and Sincerity as a Friend,
having performed many good Offices towards them
in Times of their Sicknefs, and upon every other
Opportunity. They expatiated much upon the
Evennefs of her Temper, the Regularity of her
Conduct, and the many Dangers and Hardfhips
fhe underwent, without ever fhewing the leaft
fign of Difcontent with her Situation. Thefe En-
comiums once over, the forementioned *Moody*, who
had been her Bedfellow two Nights, and was
prefent at this Difcovery, became of a fudden fo
much enamoured with her, that he propofed
to marry her, which fhe refufed, upon reflecting what a bad Husband fhe formerly had,
and who had been the Inftrument of all her Mif-
fortunes, therefore for his fake fhe refolved, in the
Mind fhe was then in, never to engage with any
Man living.

Now

Now upon the Discovery of her Sex, her Relations, and some of her intimate Friends, advised her to apply by a Petition to his Royal Highness the Duke of *Cumberland*, not doubting but that his Highness would make some proper Provision for her, as she had received so many Wounds. Upon which a Petition was drawn up, setting forth her Adventures, and the Hardships she underwent, together with the many Wounds she received, which she was the Bearer of herself, and coming where his Royal Highness then was in his Landau, accompanied by Colonel *Napier*, she delivered her Petition to his Royal Highness, and upon his perusing it, gave it to the Colonel, desiring him to enquire into the Merits. So that it is not doubted but his Royal Highness will make her some handsome Allowance, exclusive of *Chelsea* College, to which she is entitled.

Now, notwithstanding this our Heroine has at sundry Times appeared upon a publick Stage since her Return to *England*, and diverted the Auditors with a Song or two, in order to procure a little Money, wherewith to support her present necessary Expences, yet the Publick we hope will encourage her, if she should have a Benefit Play perform'd on her own Account, as an Encouragement for the many singular Adventures, and signal Deliverances from the many Perils and Dangers that environed her, and all in the Behalf of her Country: Her Merit I think is such as is sufficient to set her upon a Level with the most celebrated Ladies of antient Times. She is not to be put in the Lists with the fictitious and fabulous Stories of a *Pamella*, &c. no, her Virtues have displayed their Lustre in the remotest Corner of the World, the once fam'd *Asia*. It was here she performed such noble Deeds, as will cause her Name and Fame to be revered to latest Posterity: Here is the real *Pamella* to be found, who in the midst of thousands

of

of the Martial Gentry, preserved her Chastity by the most virtuous Stratagems that could be devised : Next behold her upon the Ocean, surrounded with Storms, Tempests and Hurricanes, every Moment expecting the watery Element should prove her Tomb ; and as an Addition to her wretched Situation, she was intermixed with the hardy resolute Tars, who soon would have batter'd down the Fort of her Virtue, had they discovered that *James Gray* was Mrs. *Hannah Snell.* See her making for fair *Asia*'s ancient Shore, with all the speed that Canvas Wings could carry her ; and going aloft and discharging the Duty of a skilful Mariner ; afterwards upon the Poop and Quarter Deck exercising her small Arms, as an able and experienced Soldier : Then when the Enemy were attacked, firing her Pontoons, brandishing her Sword, receiving dangerous Wounds, and spilling her precious Blood : If these, together with many more Circumstances, are not Virtues infinitely surpassing the Adventures and Virtues of our romantick *Pamella*, I own I am mistaken, and shall leave them to the Judgment of the impartial Reader. This is a real *Pamella* ; the other a counterfeit ; this *Pamella* is real Flesh and Blood, the other is no more than a Shadow : Therefore let this our Heroine, who is the Subject of this History, be both admired and encouraged.

I shall conclude this Subject, with observing, that notwithstanding the many Reflections thrown upon the Fair Sex on Account of their Weakness in Point of Secret, the Conduct of our Heroine in this Particular is a plain and demonstrative Proof of this Truth, that a Woman is not only capable of confining a Secret in her Bosom, but actually do so upon sundry Emergences, seeing she concealed her Sex in the midst of the greatest Dangers and Hardships ; no Difficulties, no Pains, no Terrors, nor Prospect of future Calamities, could prevail upon

G

her

her to difcover a Secret, which, if once divulged,
might have proved more fatal to her Repofe, than
all the Difficulties fhe had undergone during the
paft Courfe of her Adventures.

THE Adventures of this Female Soldier, as the
like is not to be parallelled in Hiftory, fhould never
be forgot by our *Britifh* Ladies, but whenever fa-
tirized by any of the Mafculine Gentry, they
fhould always have this Repartee ready, *Remember*
HANNAH SNELL.

I SHALL now conclude with informing the Publick, that fhe ftill continues to wear her Regimentals ; but how fhe intends to difpofe of herfelf,
or when, if ever, to change her Drefs, is more
than what fhe at prefent feems certain of.

F I N I S.

AS this Treatife was done in a Hurry from *Hannah Snell*'s own Mouth, and directly committed to the Prefs, occafioned by the Impatience of the Town to have it publifhed, it is not doubted but that fuch Part of it as appears fomewhat incorrect, will be candidly overlook'd, that, being made up in the Veracity and Fulnefs of her furprifing Adventures; the like not to be met with in the Records of Time.